This Journal Belongs to:

_____

Text copyright © 1997 by Karen Hill.
Illustrations © 1997 by Bobby Gombert.

All rights reserved. No portion of this book may be reproduced in any form without written permission from the publisher, except for brief excerpts in reviews.

Published in Nashville, Tennessee, by Tommy Nelson™, a division of Thomas Nelson, Inc. Executive Editor: Laura Minchew; Managing Editor: Beverly Phillips.

Unless otherwise indicated, Bible verses are from the *International Children's Bible, New Century Version*, copyright 1983, 1986, 1988 by Word Publishing.

Quotations marked (NCV) are from *The Holy Bible, New Century Version*, copyright 1987, 1988, 1991 by Word Publishing.

ISBN 0-8499-1453-1 (Fish cover)
ISBN 0-8499-1506-6 (Flower cover)
ISBN 0-8499-5964-0 (Bird, green cover)
ISBN 0-8499-5965-9 (Bird, pink cover)

Printed in the United States of America

99 00 01 02 RRD 9 8 7 6 5 4

My Faith Journal

WRITTEN BY
Karen Hill

ILLUSTRATED BY
Bobby Gombert

Thomas Nelson, Inc.
Nashville

From the Author

To my children
Lindsey, John, and Caitlin
for bringing such joy to my journey.

And with greatest gratitude to these dear friends:
Art, Marco, Max, Denalyn, Suzie, Judy,
Margaret-Ann, Liz, the two Jeffs, and Mama.

Karen Hill

From the Illustrator

To my God in heaven,
who has given me more strength and mercy
than I deserve, and to a loving circle of family
and friends who have always believed in me
when I didn't believe in myself.

Bobby J. Gombert

Contents

Introduction........................... vi
1. My Journey through Fear.................. 1
2. My Journey of Praise................... 4
3. My Journey Out of Confusion 7
4. My Journey When Kids Make Fun of Me 10
5. My Journey through Jealousy 13
6. My Journey in Friendship............. 16
7. My Journey through Problems 19
8. My Journey through Loneliness......... 22
9. My Journey in Courage.................. 25
10. My Journey with Kindness............... 28
11. My Journey of Prayer 31
12. My Journey in Forgiveness............ 34
13. My Journey with Patience............ 37
14. My Journey with Blessings 40
15. My Journey through Anger........... 43
16. My Journey with Laughter.............. 46
17. My Journey through Boredom.......... 49
18. My Journey in Responsibility 52
19. My Journey with Mistakes 55
20. My Journey with Pets................... 58
21. My Journey with Imagination 61
22. My Journey through Sadness 64
23. My Journey in Love 67
24. My Journey with Truth 70
25. My Journey in Respect 73
26. My Journey of Thankfulness 76
27. My Journey with Trust................ 79
28. My Journey with Promises............. 82
29. My Journey of Joy 85
30. My Faith Journey 88

Introduction

Guess who I was thinking about when I wrote this book? You! Each day, as I started writing, I said a prayer just for you. I asked God to help me think of ideas that you would enjoy writing about, as you learn to know him better and see how he works in your life. I thought about you, your family and friends, your days at school and church. I could see you playing sports and practicing your music lessons. Through it all, I feel as though you and I have become great friends.

So, friend, I hope you enjoy putting your heart into this journal. When I was your age, I always kept a journal of my thoughts. In happy times, sad times, scary times or even funny times, it was helpful to write about my feelings. Maybe you're like that, too. This journal provides a special place for all your thoughts.

As you travel these pages, remember that this is *your* book. That means there aren't any rules! No teacher is going to put a grade on any page. It's just for you.

To start, choose a subject from the table of contents about what's happening in your life. Today you may want to write about your favorite pet—there's a chapter just for that. Next week, you may hear a great joke you want to save—go to the chapter on "Laughter." If you're feeling kind of sad, turn to "My Journey through Sadness" and write down how you feel. There's no schedule to keep—you might spend a whole year filling up these pages. Just write as events in your life unfold.

This journal is meant as a keepsake. When you grow up, it will help you remember the times of your life. You may even want to share this memory book with your own kids someday. Imagine that!

Now, start writing! And have a great journaling journey of faith! As you write, keep this verse in mind: *"Go in peace. The Lord is pleased with your journey."* (Judges 18:6)

Your Friend,
Karen Hill

P. S. I'd love to hear about your Faith Journey. You can write me at Tommy Nelson™, 404 BNA Drive, Building 200, Suite 508, Nashville, TN, 37217.

1. My Journey through Fear

Sometimes life gets scary. Sometimes it's so scary I feel like crying. I wonder if I'll ever feel brave.

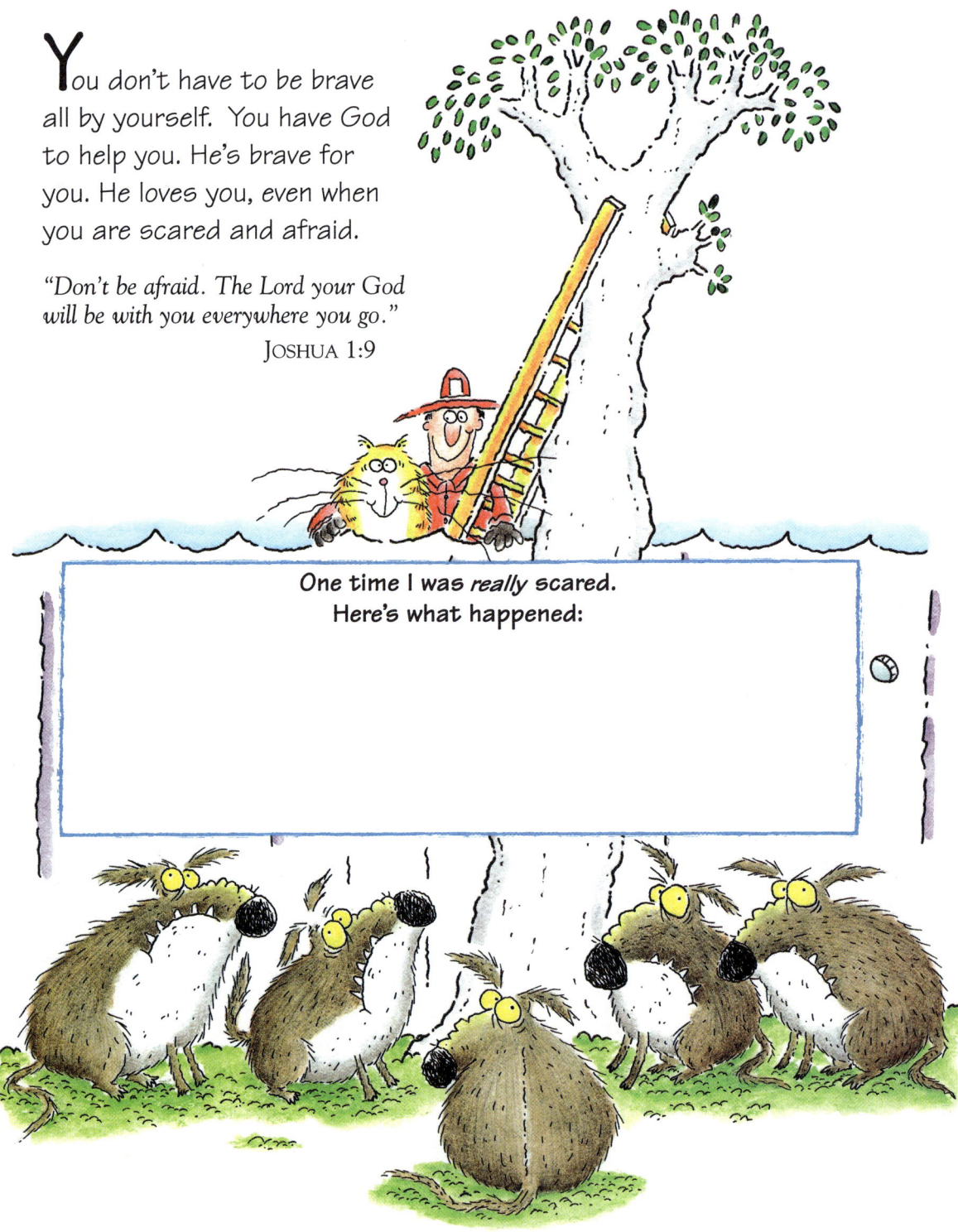

You don't have to be brave all by yourself. You have God to help you. He's brave for you. He loves you, even when you are scared and afraid.

"Don't be afraid. The Lord your God will be with you everywhere you go."
JOSHUA 1:9

One time I was *really* scared. Here's what happened:

MY JOURNEY

My list of scary things:

1.

2.

3.

4.

My list of people who help me be brave:

1.

2.

3.

4.

Someone in the Bible who was scared was Peter.
(Read Matthew 14:29–32.) This is what happened:

When I get scared, I'll think about Peter and how God helped him be brave.

2. My Journey of Praise

People are always talking about praising. What is praise anyway? Do I only praise God in church? Can I praise anywhere?

Praise is a way to show God that you are excited to be his child. It can be singing, shouting, or even clapping. Praise is kind of like prayer, but with more energy! Pray-Z-Z-Z! So, be listening, Heavenly Father, because some powerful pray-z-z-z is heading straight for heaven!

"I will praise you every day. I will praise you forever and ever."
PSALM 145:2

I like to praise God about:

MY JOURNEY

When I want to praise God quietly, I can talk to him in my heart, and this is what I say:

When I want to praise God out loud, I can sing, or jump up and down, or dance. Here's a picture of me praising God:

I can write a psalm (or praise poem) just like King David wrote in Psalms 96 and 101. Here is a praise poem just for you, Heavenly Father:

3. My Journey Out of Confusion

Being a kid is tough sometimes. Life can be confusing. You think everything's going great and then— Wham! You feel like you're in the pits.

God says we should hang onto him. He says we can count on him to pull us back up. So, next time I feel like yelling, "Help!" I'll pray. He's always ready to toss me a rope!

"The Lord God gives me my strength. He makes me like a deer, which does not stumble. He leads me safely on the steep mountains."
                                          HABAKKUK 3:19

One time I didn't know what to do. I was confused about:

MY JOURNEY

When I am confused and unsure, this is what I can do:

I can ask this person for advice:

Next time I get confused, I'll read:

John 14:27

Romans 8:28

1 Corinthians 14:33

4. My Journey When Kids Make Fun of Me

Sometimes other kids make fun of me. I don't know what to do when someone teases me about my size, or my clothes, or the way I act.

When that happens, remember what Jesus said about people who make fun of you: "Be kind to them." Even if it doesn't change the things they say, you'll feel stronger, knowing that you're pleasing God!

"Be kind and loving to each other. Forgive each other just as God forgave you in Christ."

EPHESIANS 4:32

Someone made fun of me one time. This is what he (she) said:

MY JOURNEY

I want to stop thinking bad thoughts about this person. Something good I can say about him (her) is:

Here's what I can *do* to show kindness to this person:

Each day this week, I will pray this prayer:

Dear God,

I need your help. Please help me to remember that you want me to be kind to _____. Help me stop being angry at _____. Will you give me the courage to be kind? And please help _____ be kind to me, too. Amen.

5. My Journey through Jealousy

There are kids who are smarter, better-looking, funnier, stronger, more athletic, and more talented than I am. I know it's wrong to feel jealous, but it's hard not to!

Wait a minute! Instead of thinking about *them*, remember that God made *you* just the way he wanted you to be. He chose the color of your hair and eyes. He decided how tall you would be. He gave you special talents and abilities. When you start to feel jealous of someone else, remember that *you* are God's dream come true.

"God has made us what we are."
EPHESIANS 2:10

Once I felt jealous because:

MY JOURNEY

This is how being jealous makes me feel:

Next time I feel jealous, I'll remember that God made me special in these ways:

1.

2.

3.

4.

5.

Jealousy can cause trouble. In the Bible, some brothers were jealous of their brother Joseph. See what happened when the brothers were jealous (read Genesis 37).

6. My Journey in Friendship

A friend is a special blessing from God. A friend is someone who likes me, even when I mess up! With my friend, I can be serious or funny, share secrets, and dream dreams.

You and your friend can talk about God together. What a great gift a friend can be!

"My children, we should love people not only with words and talk, but by our actions of caring."

1 JOHN 3:18, NCV

Here are some ways I can be a good friend:

MY JOURNEY

My special friend is:

This is what we like to do together:

Jesus had many friends. Some of his special friends were Mary, Martha, and Lazarus. (Read John 11: 1–44.) Write down how they showed their friendship for Jesus:

And this is how Jesus showed them he was their friend:

7. My Journey through Problems

Just when things are going great, up comes a PROBLEM! Sometimes my problem seems big enough to swallow me up! And sometimes I wonder where God is? Does he know about my problem? Does he care?

You bet he does! And God is always ready to help. Together, God and you can turn those big problems into little ripples.

"The Lord took me to a safe place. Because he delights in me, he saved me."
                                    PSALM 18:19

I remember a time when a problem seemed too big for me. It was when:

MY JOURNEY

This is how God helps me with my problems:

The next time I have a BIG problem, I'll read these verses to help me remember that God can help me:

"People, t_____ God all the time. Tell him all your p_____.

God is our p_____." (Psalm 62:8)

"I pour out my p_____ to him (God). I tell him my t_____.

When I am a_____, you, Lord, know the way out."

(Psalm 142:2–3)

8. My Journey through Loneliness

Say the word *lonely* and it sounds so sad. Look at the word *lonely* and see why. Inside *lone*ly is the word *one*. See it? Right there in the middle. When I feel lonely, it's because I feel all alone. Am I the only ONE who ever feels lonely?

I should remember that even Jesus sometimes felt lonely. There were times when his friends didn't believe in him. Sometimes his friends didn't even admit they were his friends. Once, his friends ran away and hid from him! When you feel lonely, talk to God about your feelings. When no one on earth understands, remember that you are not alone. There is ONE in heaven who is listening!

"Give all your worries to him [God], because he cares for you."
1 PETER 5:7

I felt lonely when:

MY JOURNEY

Some people who help me get over my loneliness are:

This is what they do to help me:

Next time I feel lonely, this is what I will do:

If I am lonely, I'll read these verses:

2 Corinthians 1:3–4

Colossians 1:11

1 Peter 1:5–7

Isaiah 43:5

9. My Journey in Courage

It takes courage to do the right thing. I'm learning the difference between right and wrong. But I'm also learning that sometimes it's tough to do what I know is right! I sure could use some courage.

Hang in there! God doesn't expect you to do it alone. And he doesn't expect you to be perfect. But he does expect you to try your best. When you're trying to do what's right, use the tools he's given you.

"Be strong in the Lord and in his great power. Wear the full armor of God. Wear God's armor so that you can fight against the devil's evil tricks."

EPHESIANS 6:10–11

I was courageous when:

MY JOURNEY

Almost every day I have to choose between right and wrong. These are some *right* choices I made recently:

1.

2.

3.

4.

When I need courage, I can read about how God made Peter and John courageous. (Read Acts 4:1–13.) Remembering Peter and John gives me courage because:

"Wait for the Lord's help. Be strong and brave and wait for the Lord's help." (Psalm 27:14)

10. My Journey with Kindness

Sometimes I'm not sure how to show kindness to others. Will they like what I do for them? Will they be embarrassed that I know something's wrong?
Well, God says we should "serve each other with love" (Galatians 5:13).

You know, it's a funny thing about being kind to others—it makes *me* feel better, too!

"God is fair. He will not forget the work you did and the love you showed for him by helping his people."

Hebrews 6:10

Some people who have been kind to me:

MY JOURNEY

I want to be like _____ because this person has a kind heart. I can see this because:

I know someone who could use a little kindness. Here are some ways I can be kind to this person:

Jesus told a story about a kind man (Luke 10:30–37). If I could write the end of the story, this is what the hurt man would say to the one who was kind:

For more about kindness, read Matthew 25:34–40.

11. My Journey of Prayer

How can I be sure God knows what I need? Is he interested in things like helping me get along with my brother or sister?

Yes, he's interested all right. In fact, God cares so much about you that he created prayer. Prayer is like a phone line straight to heaven—no answering machine, no busy signal. He's always ready to listen.

"The Lord our God comes near when we pray to him."
DEUTERONOMY 4:7

Dear God,

Thank you for_____

_____.

I love you because_____

_____.

I'm sorry about_____

_____.

MY JOURNEY

My favorite time to pray is:

When I pray, I thank God for:

Someone who always prays for me is:

The Bible tells about many people who prayed.

Matthew 14:23

Luke 5:16

Luke 6:28

12. My Journey in Forgiveness

Feelings get hurt, rumors get started, someone gets left out. It's hard to forgive these things. Does God expect me to forgive someone who treated me this way?

God understands that forgiving others is hard. But it's easier when we remember that he forgives us! When I disobey, he forgives me. When I forget to talk to him, he forgives me anyway! When I remember how good God is to me, it's easier for me to forgive someone else.

"Do not be angry with each other, but forgive each other. If someone does wrong to you, then forgive him. Forgive each other because the Lord forgave you."

Colossians 3:13

I need to forgive someone. This is why:

MY JOURNEY

(Check the box)
☐ One time I forgave someone for _____.
☐ I haven't forgiven this person yet, but I'm praying about it.

I needed forgiveness one time, too. This is what I did:

After I forgave someone I felt:

During my study time, I can read these verses about forgiveness:

Psalm 86:5

Micah 7:18

Matthew 6:12–15

1 John 1:9

13. My Journey with Patience

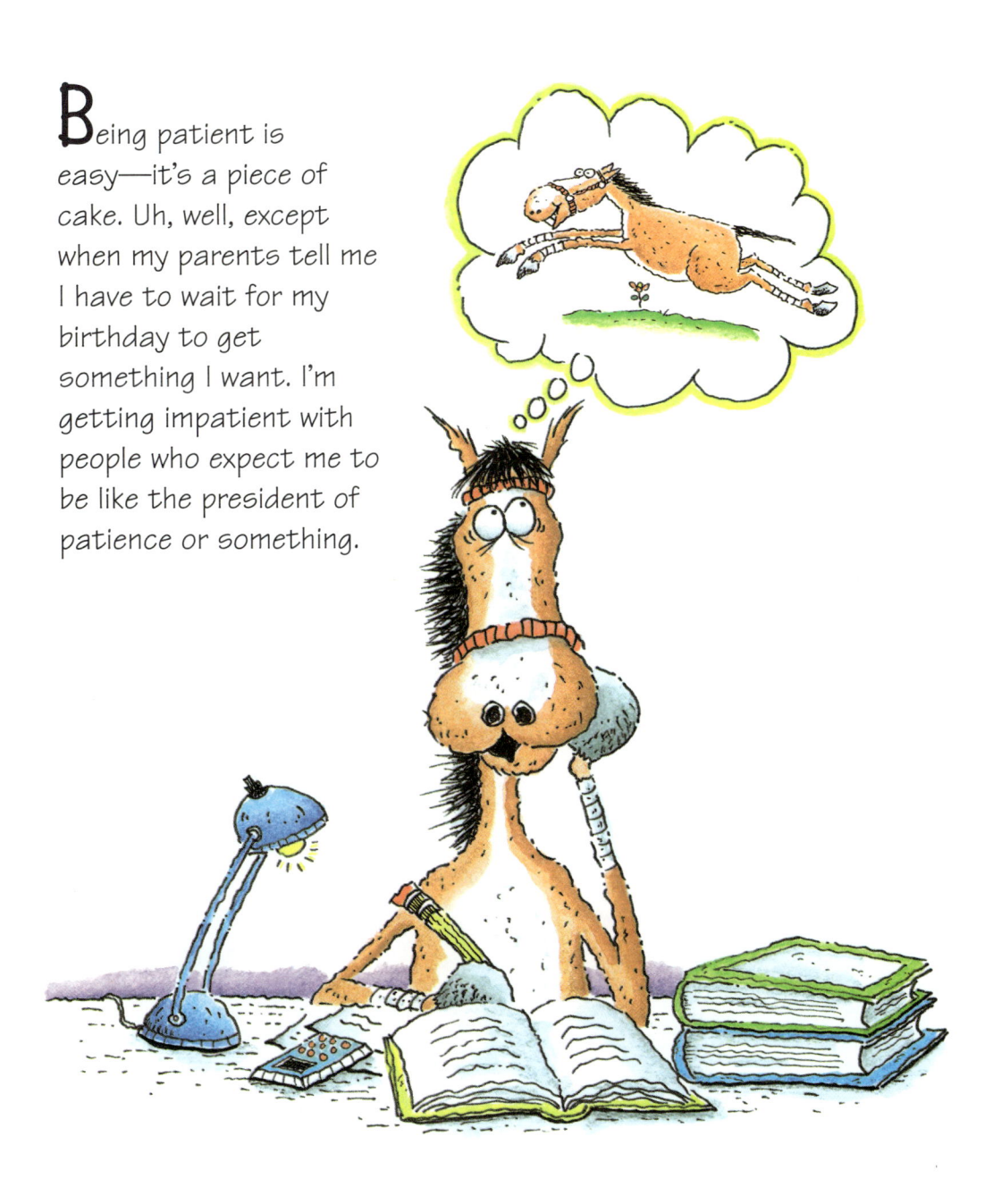

Being patient is easy—it's a piece of cake. Uh, well, except when my parents tell me I have to wait for my birthday to get something I want. I'm getting impatient with people who expect me to be like the president of patience or something.

Okay, here's the plan. God says I can be patient. He is right. It may take a while, but I'll try to be more patient with myself and others.

"Always be humble and gentle. Be patient and accept each other with love."
EPHESIANS 4:2

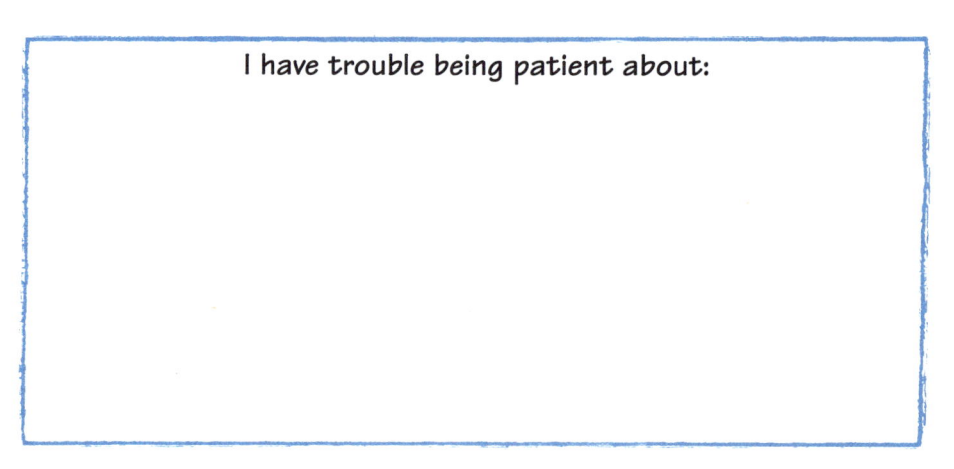

I have trouble being patient about:

MY JOURNEY

It's hard to be patient about:

Someone I know who is usually patient is:

This is how patient people act:

Someone in the Bible who was patient was:

During my study time, I can read these Bible verses about patience:

Romans 15:5

1 Corinthians 13:4

James 1:4

14. My Journey with Blessings

God blesses me in many ways. He blesses me with family and home, and with teachers, friends, food, clothes . . . Our heavenly Father is smart. He knows what I need even before I ask for it!

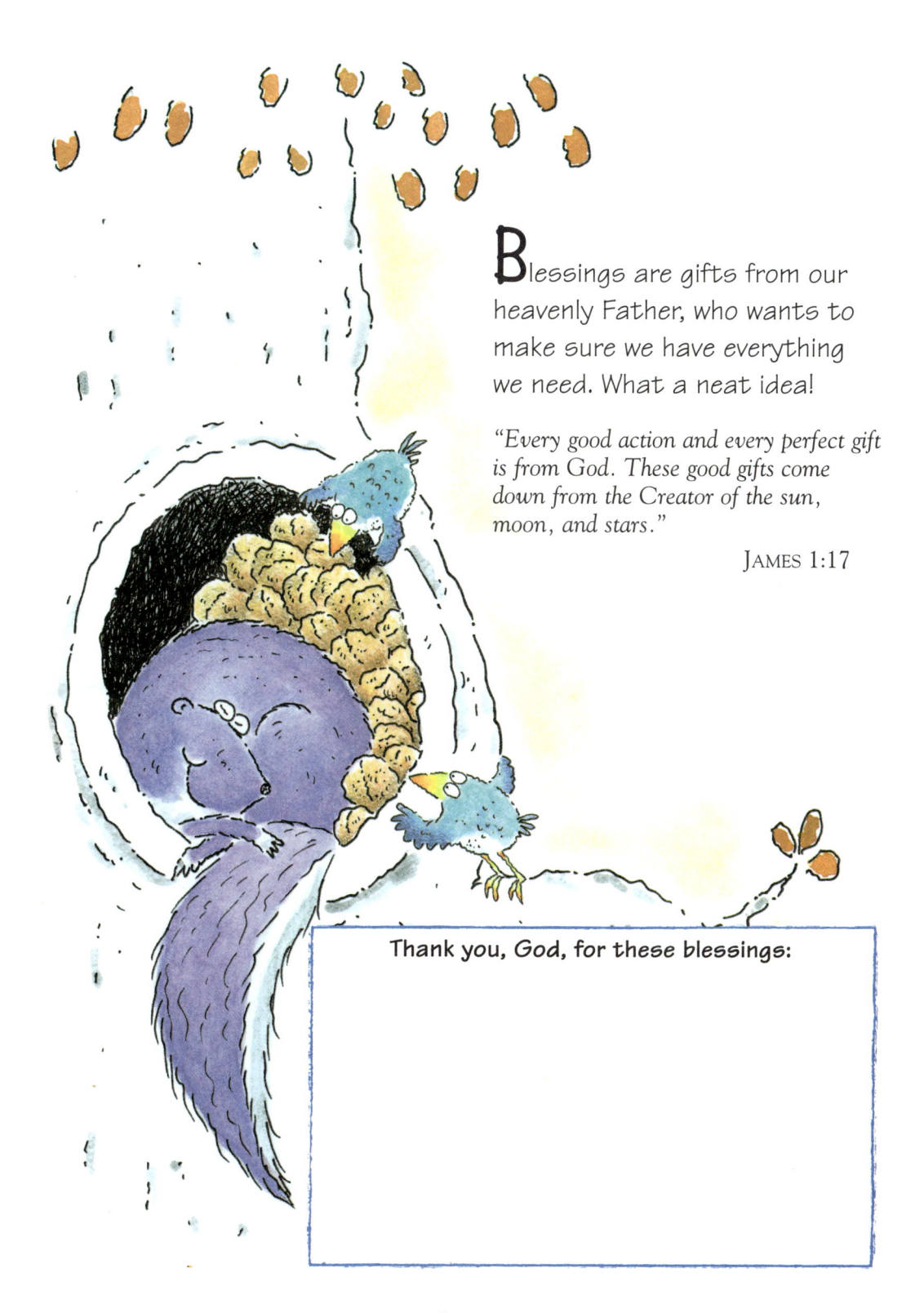

Blessings are gifts from our heavenly Father, who wants to make sure we have everything we need. What a neat idea!

"Every good action and every perfect gift is from God. These good gifts come down from the Creator of the sun, moon, and stars."

JAMES 1:17

Thank you, God, for these blessings:

MY JOURNEY

If I could give a blessing to God, this is what it would be:

Here's a picture that shows a blessing God gave me:

During my study time, I can read these scriptures about blessings:

Psalm 126:3

Psalm 65: 9–13

Luke 12:22–31

15. My Journey through Anger

I get so mad sometimes I feel like I'll explode! I know anger can be dangerous. But how do I calm down?

Try to calm down by exercising or counting to ten before you speak. This will help you control your anger rather than your anger controlling you. If anger gets out of control, someone could get hurt—and it could be you!

"Always be willing to listen and slow to speak. Do not become angry easily. Anger will not help you live a good life as God wants."
JAMES 1:19–20

I really got angry one time. This is what made me mad:

MY JOURNEY

This is how I handled my anger:

When I get angry, I'll try to control myself this way:

If I have trouble controlling my anger, I'll go to this person for help:

God doesn't want his children to be angry. These are some important verses to remember:

"Don't become m_____ q_____, because getting a_____ is f_____." (Ecclesiastes 7:9)

"Do not be b_____ or a_____ or m_____. Never shout a_____ or say things to h_____ others. Never do anything e_____." (Ephesians 4:31)

16. My Journey with Laughter

When my funny bone gets tickly,
I start feeling giggly!

First, it's just a tiny "tee-hee,"
Then it grows to a smile—goodness, I feel silly!
Oops, there it goes . . . it simply won't stop.
It's a roaring laugh—Ha! Ha! I think I'm gonna pop!

"Now my children, listen to me. Those who follow my ways are happy."

PROVERBS 8:32

I always laugh about:

MY JOURNEY

Here's my favorite joke:

In my family, the funniest person is:

This is how he makes me laugh:

I think God made laughter because:

"A happy heart is like a continual feast."
(Proverbs 15:15 NCV)

17. My Journey through Boredom

"Hey, Mom, I'm bored!" (Have you ever said that?) When you talk about being bored, grown-ups probably say something like *(check the ones you've heard)*:

☐ Find something to do.

☐ Go read a book.

☐ Clean up your room.

☐ Quit fussing!

☐ When I was your age, I had so many chores, there wasn't time to get bored.

Am I the only one who ever gets bored?

Here's a little secret about being bored (now listen carefully)—it usually happens when we're busy thinking about ourselves instead of others.

"I have learned to be satisfied with the things I have and with everything that happens. . . . I have learned the secret of being happy at any time in everything that happens."
PHILIPPIANS 4:11, 12

I get bored when:

MY JOURNEY

Next time I feel bored, I'll:

☐ Draw a card for a sick person I know.

☐ Offer to help someone in my family with a chore.

☐ Call a friend to say hi.

☐ Write in *My Faith Journal*.

☐ Do a secret kindness for a neighbor.

(You finish the list):

_____

_____

_____

_____

This is my favorite way to get over being bored:

18. My Journey in Responsibility

Grown-ups always use the word: *r-e-s-p-o-n-s-i-b-i-l-i-t-y*. Whew! I get tired just saying it! As I get older, it seems I am asked to be more responsible. Does this ever stop?

No. *Responsibility* is an important word to understand. *Responsibility* means "I respond to a situation with my ability." It means "You can count on me!" As I get older, my ability increases and so do my responsibilities. God made each of us different. He wants me to be responsible for the special job he has in mind for me:

"Some things are used for special purposes, and others are made for ordinary jobs."

2 Timothy 2:20

I am responsible about:

MY JOURNEY

The grown-ups in my life want me to learn to be responsible for:

When someone gives me a job to do, here's how they are helping me learn responsiblity:

Here's a list of my responsibilities that no one has to remind me to do:

In the Bible a young boy named David learned responsibility. First, David was a shepherd. He learned to be responsible for his sheep. Then God made him a king, and he was responsible for leading people. (Read Psalm 78:70–71.)

19. My Journey with Mistakes

I never ~~maik misteaks~~ make mistakes. Yeah, right. Doesn't everyone make mistakes?

Absolutely! But doing something dumb shouldn't make you feel awful. Remember who loves you, mistakes and all. Your heavenly Father! (Besides, he can help you undo your mistakes (just talk to him about it.)

"God does not see the same way people see. People look at the outside of a person, but the Lord looks at the heart."

1 Samuel 16:7

I made a big mistake one time.
Here's what happened:

MY JOURNEY

The worst thing about making mistakes is:

I saw a grown-up make a mistake one time. It was when:

Someone once said, "Mistakes are lessons in the school of life." That means:

A lot of Bible stories are about people making mistakes. Someone who made a big mistake was Saul (who was also called Paul), before he became a Christian (read Acts 9:1–2). This is what he did:

This is how Saul learned from his mistake (read Acts 9:3-9):

20. My Journey with Pets

Pets are special friends. They know how to say "I love you" without using words! I can tell a lot about what my pets are thinking by the way they act.

All the animals in the world belong to God. Thanks, God, for letting me take care of your pets!

God says, . . . "Every animal of the forest is already mine. The cattle on a thousand hills are mine. I know every bird on the mountains. Every living thing in the fields is mine."

PSALM 50:7, 10–11

I think the best pet in the whole world is:

MY JOURNEY

I have a pet _____. (If you don't have a pet, write about a pet you'd like to have.) My pet does many things. Some of the things my pet does are:

When my pet does this, I know he loves me:

This is how I take care of my pet:

If I could be somebody's pet, I would like to be a:

"A good man takes care of his animals."
(Proverbs 12:10)

21. My Journey with Imagination

When my brain takes a vacation
To the land of imagination,
I'm full of fascination—
What will be my destination?

It could be any location
Just waiting for exploration.
My thoughts are my transportation.
Imagination! What jubilation!

"Praise the Lord. He alone is great! He is greater than heaven and earth."
Psalm 148:13

I love to imagine . . .

MY JOURNEY

In my imagination, I can be a _____. This is the name I use for my imaginary character: _____. My make-believe character and I do this:

In my imagination, I am a cloud. This is what I look like:

In my imagination, I am Jesus' next-door neighbor. We are friends and we play together this way:

Thank you, Dear God, for giving me the gift of imagination!

22. My Journey through Sadness

Sometimes I feel *really* sad. If God loves me, then why don't I feel happy all the time? Why do bad things happen? Will this feeling go away?

Sooner or later, sad things happen in everyone's life. Maybe someone you love is hurt or even dies, or maybe you are hurt. When bad things happen to people we love, we feel like our hearts will break. And when that happens, it's hard to stop being sad. God promises us that sad times will not last forever. Even in really bad times, God is with us, helping fix our broken hearts. And when we get through the sad time, he makes us stronger, so that we can help others be strong. God makes this promise to people who love him:

> *"I am the one who comforts you."*
> Isaiah 51:12

I felt sad when:

MY JOURNEY

When I feel sad, I . . .

1. . . . go to a quiet place by myself. This is my favorite quiet place:

2. . . . talk to someone who is wise. This is my favorite wise person:

3. . . . get some exercise. This is what I can do:

4. . . . read and pray. This is my prayer when I am sad:

Other things that help me when I'm sad:

Jesus knows what it's like to be sad. One of his best friends died. (Read John 11:17–44.)

When you feel sad, remember this verse:

"The Lord God will wipe away every tear from every face." (Isaiah 25:8)

23. My Journey in Love

Have you heard someone say, "He's got an ATTITUDE"? Well, guess what? Here's a good attitude to have: loving others, just like Jesus did.

Love isn't just hugs, kisses, or a gushy, mushy, fuzzy feeling. It's not valentines and candy. Love is caring about others, being good to others (even when they're not so lovable). You show your love to your family and friends by how you treat them. Love is a great attitude!

"Love your neighbor as you love yourself."
GALATIANS 5:14

"Love each other deeply with all your heart."
1 PETER 1:22

This is what love means to me:

MY JOURNEY

God's definition of love (read Romans 12:9–14 for the answers): "Your love must be r_____. Hate what is e_____. Hold on to what is g_____. Love each other like b_____ and s_____. . . . Be j_____ because you have hope. . . . Wish good for those who do b_____ things to you."

God has given me many people to love. Here are their names and something that I love about them:

Here is a list of people and the things I can do to show my love for them.

For more about love, I can read 1 Corinthians 13:4–7.

24. My Journey with Truth

Sometimes it's hard to be truthful—especially when I know the truth will hurt or disappoint someone.

Next time you're tempted to tell a lie, think about how you feel when someone is untruthful to you. Ask God to help you tell the truth, even if it's going to hurt a bit.

"We show that we are servants of God by living a pure life, by our understanding, by our patience, and by our kindness. . . . by speaking the truth, and by God's power."

2 CORINTHIANS 6:6–7

Once I told a lie. It was about:

MY JOURNEY

It's important to tell the truth because:

It's sometimes hard to tell the truth about:

I heard someone tell a lie. This is what happened:

What the Bible says about truth:

"The Lord hates those who tell lies. But he is pleased with those who do what they promise." (Proverbs 12:22)

"Truth will last forever. But lies last only for a moment." (Proverbs 12:19)

25. My Journey in Respect

When I show respect for others, I am showing respect for God, too. After all, we are all his children. Fathers want their children treated well!

Some ways I show respect:

Respect includes being considerate of someone else's feelings; showing honor to someone else; or letting someone know you appreciate him.

"Show respect for all people. Love the brothers and sisters of God's family. Respect God."

1 Peter 2:17

MY JOURNEY

I felt good when someone showed respect to me. This is my story:

This is how I show Jesus that I respect him:

"Respect Christ as the holy Lord in your hearts. Always be ready to answer everyone who asks you to explain about the hope you have. But answer in a gentle way and with respect."
(1 Peter 3:15–16)

26. My Journey of Thankfulness

I'm bringing a heart-gift of thankfulness to God. It is a one-of-a-kind package wrapped in my praise and tied with my love for all he has done for me. I hope you like my gift, Father!

God knows of your gift. He can see it tucked away inside you. He knows it's a special present just for him.

"Thank the Lord because he is good. His love continues forever."
　　　　　　　　　　　　1 Chronicles 16:34

If I could give my heavenly Father a gift, it would be:

MY JOURNEY

Write a thank-you letter to God. Just open your heart and pour your thankfulness out on this page.

"God, we thank you. We thank you because you are near."
(Psalm 75:1)

"You are my God, and I will thank you. You are my God, and I will praise your greatness. Thank the Lord because he is good. His love continues forever."
(Psalms 118:28–29)

27. My Journey with Trust

When I was little, I trusted God. Now that I'm older, I'll trust him, too. All my life, I will depend on God to take care of me. He always has, and he always will!

Trusting God means believing that he knows all about you and will take care of what you need. How could you get along without him?

"Lord, I give myself to you. My God, I trust you. . . . I trust you all day long."
Psalm 25:1,5

I trust God because:

MY JOURNEY

Trusting God means feeling safe with him. It's like trusting the grown-ups in my life. A grown-up I trust is:

This is how I know I can trust him or her:

And this is how _____ knows I am trustworthy, too:

"The Lord is my strength and shield. I trust him, and he helps me." (Psalm 28:7)

"Depend on the Lord. Trust him, and he will take care of you." (Psalm 37:5)

28. My Journey with Promises

Promises, promises. Easy to make. Easy to keep? Well . . . I have trouble keeping some promises.

God wants his children to keep their promises, just as he keeps his promises to them. A promise is a little piece of yourself that you give away. A promise is a beautiful thing!

". . . Jesus called us by his glory and goodness. Through his glory and goodness, he gave us the very great and rich gifts he promised us."

2 PETER 1:3–4

Here is a promise I will always keep:

MY JOURNEY

Someone made a special promise to me once. This is the promise:

I had a hard time keeping a promise one time. This is why:

The best promise I can make to God is:

29. My Journey of Joy

I know a secret about being one of God's children: He wants all of his children to have fun—and that includes me! He wants me to smile, laugh, and to be full of joy and happiness!

Why does God want you to have fun? Because he loves you, and because your joy reminds other people that you love the God who promised that you would one day live with him forever. Hooray!

"Happy are the people whose God is the Lord."
                                        PSALM 144:15

I am joyful because:

MY JOURNEY

This is how I show my joy to the world:

Here's a picture of me feeling joyful:

"But I will still be glad in the Lord. I will rejoice in God my Savior." (Habakkuk 3:18)

30. My Faith Journey

Don't think that just because you're young, you can't understand what faith is. Jesus loved kids like you so much that he told all the grown-ups they should be *more like you!*

Faith is believing with all your heart that Jesus is God's son, and that he came to earth to save all of us, so that someday we'll live in heaven with him forever!

"You have not seen Christ, but still you love him. You cannot see him now, but you believe in him. You are filled with a joy that cannot be explained. And that joy is full of glory."

1 PETER 1:8

I believe that Jesus is the son of God.

_____

(Sign your name here.)

MY JOURNEY

Having faith in God means that (check all you believe):

☐ I have given him my heart forever.

☐ I want to learn more about him.

☐ I will praise his name every day.

☐ I will live a life that makes him smile!

This is the story of how I learned about Jesus:

As I continue my journey of faith, these verses will remind me that God is always there to help me along the way:

"Have faith in the Lord your God. Then you will stand strong." (2 Chronicles 20:20)

". . . You are all children of God through faith in Christ Jesus." (Galatians 3:26)